Air Fryer Grill Cookbook

Fry, Grill, Bake, And Roast For Your Family Using Your Air Fryer Grill. Stay Healthy and Enjoy Tasty and Mouthwatering Recipes.

Table of Contents

Introduction

The air fryer is a new way to cook conveniently without all of the oil and grease. The recipes include many dishes that you already love but are just as easy as using your regular stove. They are also healthier than fried foods because they use a small amount of oil or no oil at all, which means you can feed your family without guilt. Some people think that this system is weird or hard, but really, it's just an innovative way to cook food. Here are the top six reasons why you should switch to an air fryer to get healthier meals fast:

You can cook your favorite dishes without frying! You can be eating healthy without having to do any extra work. Your food will not taste like fried food, which is always a plus for kids. Your food will not stick to the tray or sides of the fryer because it uses less oil, so you don't have to worry about scraping it off or cleaning up grease. There are many different types of air fryers, so you can pick the one best suited for your needs. Most air fryers have many safety features to keep them from overheating and turning themselves off, as well as automatic timers to keep food from burning.

The recipes in this book will help you create scrumptious meals without all the rich and heavy oil. It has an entire table of contents to help you with finding the recipes that are perfect for your needs. On top of that, it has an ingredient sector for you to know what you are cooking with so you can make sure your family is eating healthy and happy. You won't need to worry about avoiding processed foods with these recipes because all of them are homemade!

Want to get your hands on some delicious air fry recipes that won't bust the budget? This cookbook is what you need. It features 600+ recipes from a variety of cuisines, which will please any taste. Whether you're looking for something different to cook breakfast, lunch, or dinner, you'll find it in this book. Or, if you are ready to try something new for dinner tonight, you'll find that one in this book. You might even throw in a few of the side dishes as well.

All recipes are based on using air fryers, but some can be adapted to regular ovens or slow cookers. That's what makes this book so versatile. It makes cooking easier by eliminating some of the stress that you might otherwise go through when cooking with your stove and oven. So, whether you are looking for comfort food, or something more exotic, you'll find it in this book. Plus, all recipes are easy to follow and your family will enjoy that.

The best air fryers can replace most conventional cooking appliances. Air fryers, which are often called convection ovens or extractors, will quickly replace your stovetop and even your electric kettle. We've gathered the most popular models in this guide and will help you find the one that fits your needs and home-cooking style. Except for a few fairly large models, air fryers are usually small enough to fit in most kitchens. So, whether you're just getting started or have been a chef for years, an air fryer can help you cook up healthier versions of your favorite foods. When it comes to health, air-frying may be more beneficial than most people think. Air frying uses much less oil than ordinary frying while leaving behind fewer unhealthy fats and other impurities. It's also a quick and awesome way to cook up healthy sides like roasted potatoes, grilled vegetables, or even fruit.

Air-frying also preserves food's texture better than conventional frying, making air-fried dishes like French fries less prone to become soggy. When you fry a potato in regular fat, the potato becomes soft and mushy. This results from the way fat moves water out of the food.

CHAPTER 1:

Vegetable, Vegetarian and Side Dishes Recipes

1.   Mixed Veggies Combo

Preparation Time: 7 minutes

Cooking time: 18 minutes

Servings: 4

Ingredients:

- 1 cup baby carrots

- 1 cup broccoli florets

- 1 cup cauliflower florets

- 1 tbsp. olive oil

- 1 tbsp. Italian seasoning

- Salt and ground black pepper to taste

Directions:

1. In a bowl, add all the listed ingredients, then toss to coat thoroughly.

2. Place the vegetables in the air fryer basket.

3. Place the roasting pan on a lower rack to catch the drips.

4. Select AIR FRY and then adjust the temperature to 380°F and time to 18 minutes. Press START.

5. When ready, serve immediately.

Nutrition:

- Calories: 66

- Fat: 7 g

- Carbs: 7 g

- Protein: 4 g

2.   Cheesy Cauliflower Fritters

Preparation Time: 10 minutes

Cooking time: 7 minutes

Servings: 8

Ingredients:

- ½ cup chopped parsley

- 1 cup Italian breadcrumbs

- 1/3 cup shredded mozzarella cheese

- 1/3 cup shredded sharp cheddar cheese

- 1 egg

- 2 minced garlic cloves

- 3 chopped scallions

- 1 head of cauliflower

Directions:

1. Preparing the ingredients: Cut the cauliflower up into florets. Wash well and pat dry. Place into a food processor and pulse 20-30 seconds till it looks like rice.

2. Place the cauliflower rice in a bowl and mix with pepper, salt, egg, cheeses, breadcrumbs, garlic, and scallions.

3. With hands, form 15 patties of the mixture. Add more breadcrumbs if needed.

4. Air Frying. With olive oil, spritz patties, and place into your Cuisinart air fryer oven in a single layer. Set temperature to 390°F, and set time to 7 minutes, flipping after 7 minutes.

Nutrition:

- Calories: 209

- Fat: 17 g

- Protein: 6 g

- Sugar: 5 g

3.   Jalapeño Poppers

Preparation Time: 7 minutes

Cooking time: 10 minutes

Servings: 4

Ingredients:

- 16 whole fresh jalapeños

- 1 cup nonfat refried beans

- 1 cup shredded Monterey Jack

- 1 scallion, sliced

- 1 tsp. salt, divided

- ¼ cup all-purpose flour

- 2 large eggs

- ½ cup fine cornmeal

- Olive oil cooking spray

Directions:

1. Slice each jalapeño lengthwise on one side.

2. Place the jalapeños side by side in a microwave-safe bowl and microwave them for 5 minutes until they are slightly soft.

3. Mix refried beans, scallions, ½ tsp. salt and cheese in a bowl.

4. Once your jalapeños are softened, you can scoop out the seeds and add 1 tbsp. of your refried bean mixture on each jalapeño.

5. Press the jalapeño closed around the filling.

6. Beat your eggs in a small bowl and place your flour in a separate bowl. In a third bowl, mix your cornmeal and the remaining salt.

7. Roll each pepper in the flour, then the egg, and finally in the cornmeal.

8. Place the peppers on a flat surface and coat them with a cooking spray; olive oil cooking spray is suggested.

9. Pour into the oven rack. Place the rack on the middle shelf of the Smart Air Fryer Oven.

10. Select AIR FRY. Set temperature to 400°F, and set time to 5 minutes. Press START/CANCEL to begin.

11. Turn each pepper and then cook for another 5 minutes.

12. Once done, transfer to a plate. Serve hot.

Nutrition:

- Calories: 244

- Fat: 12 g

- Fiber: 4 g

- Protein: 12 g

4.   Air Fried Cauliflower Rice

Preparation Time: 7 minutes

Cooking time: 20 minutes

Servings: 4

Ingredients:

Round 1:

- 1 tsp. turmeric

- 1 cup diced carrot

- ½ cup diced onion

- 2 tbsp. low-sodium soy sauce

- ½ block of extra firm tofu

Round 2:

- ½ cup frozen peas

- 2 minced garlic cloves

- ½ cup chopped broccoli

- 1 tbsp. minced ginger

- 1 tbsp. rice vinegar

- 1½ tsp. sesame oil

- 2 tbsp. reduced-sodium soy sauce

- 3 cups riced cauliflower

Directions:

1. Preheat the Smart Air Fryer Oven to 370°F.

2. Crumble tofu in a large bowl and toss with all the listed ingredients in Round

3. Transfer the tofu mixture to a baking dish. Place the baking dish in the Smart Air Fryer Oven cooking basket.

4. Select AIR FRY. Set the temperature to 370°F, set the time to 10 minutes, and cook 10 minutes, making sure to shake once.

5. In another bowl, toss ingredients from Round 2 together.

6. Add Round 2 mixture to the cooked tofu mixture and cook for another 10 minutes, ensuring to shake every 5 minutes. Enjoy!

Nutrition:

- Calories: 67 Fat: 8 g Protein: 3 g

5.   Brussels Sprouts Salad

Preparation Time: 15 minutes

Cooking time: 15 minutes

Servings: 4

Ingredients:

For Salad:

- 1-pound fresh medium Brussels sprouts, trimmed and halved vertically

- 3 teaspoons olive oil

- Salt and ground black pepper, as required

- 2 apples, cored and chopped

- 1 red onion, sliced

- 4 cups lettuce, torn

For Dressing:

- 2 tablespoons extra-virgin olive oil

- 2 tablespoons fresh lemon juice

- 1 tablespoon apple cider vinegar

- 1 tablespoon maple syrup

- 1 teaspoon Dijon mustard

- Salt and ground black pepper, as required

Directions:

1. For Brussels sprouts: in a bowl, add the Brussels sprout, oil, salt, and black pepper and toss to coat well.

2. Spread the Brussels sprouts on a baking pan.

3. Select "Air Fry" of Iconites Air Fryer Toaster Oven and then adjust the temperature to 360 degrees F.

4. Set the timer for 15 minutes and press "Start" to preheat.

5. After preheating, insert the baking pan in the oven.

6. Flip the Brussels sprout once halfway through.

7. When cooking time is complete, remove the baking pan from the oven.

8. Transfer the Brussels sprouts onto a plate and set them aside to cool slightly.

9. In a serving bowl, mix the Brussels sprouts, apples, onion, and lettuce.

10. For the dressing: in a bowl, add all the ingredients and beat until well combined.

11. Place the dressing over salad and gently stir to combine.

12. Serve immediately.

Nutrition:

- Calories: 235 Total Fat: 13 g

- Saturated Fat: 7 g Cholesterol: 0 mg

- Sodium: 88 mg

- Total Carbs: 35 g

- Fiber: 8 g

- Sugar: 23 g

- Protein: 9 g

6.   Buttered Cauliflower

Preparation Time: 7 minutes

Cooking time: 15 minutes **Servings:** 4

Ingredients:

- 1 lb. cauliflower head, cut into florets

- 1 tbsp. butter, melted

- ½ tsp. red pepper flakes, crushed

- Salt and ground black pepper to taste

Directions:

1. In a bowl, add all the listed ingredients and toss to coat thoroughly.

2. Place the cauliflower in the air fryer basket.

3. Select AIR FRY and then adjust the temperature to 400°F. Set the

   timer for 15 minutes and press START.

4. When ready, serve immediately.

Nutrition:

- Calories: 55 Fat: 3 g Carbs: 1 g Protein: 3 g

CHAPTER 2:

Breakfast and Brunch Recipes

7.   Hearty Vegetarian Quesadillas

Preparation Time: 10 minutes

Cooking time: 12 minutes

Servings: 2

Ingredients:

- 2 tablespoons vegetable oil

- ¼ onion, diced

- ½ cup canned whole corn kernels, strained

- ½ cup canned black beans, strained

- 1/8 teaspoon kosher salt

- 1/8 teaspoon black pepper

- 1 teaspoon taco seasoning

- ¼ lime, juiced

- 2 medium-sized flour tortillas

- ½ cup queso Chihuahua (quesadilla cheese) or mozzarella cheese, grated

Directions:

1. Place vegetable oil, onion, corn, and black beans in a skillet over medium heat. Sauté for 5 minutes.

2. Add salt, pepper, taco seasoning, and lime juice to the skillet and cook for 3 minutes.

3. Select the Bake function on the COSORI Air Fryer Toaster Oven, set the time to 4 minutes and temperature to 450°F, then press Start/Cancel to preheat.

4. Place the bean mix on 1 of the tortillas, leaving a 1-inch border.

5. Sprinkle cheese on top of the bean mix, then place the remaining tortilla on top.

6. Place quesadilla on the food tray, then insert food tray at mid-position in the preheated air fryer toaster oven. Press Start/Cancel.

7. Cut quesadillas into 4 pieces and serve with guacamole, sour cream, or your favorite salsa.

Nutrition:

- Calories: 361

- Total Fat: 11 g

- Total Carbs: 44 g

- Protein: 12 g

8.   Breakfast Ham Omelet

Preparation Time: 10 minutes

Cooking time: 10 minutes

Servings: 2

Ingredients:

- 3 large eggs

- 100g ham, cut into small pieces ¼ cup milk

- ¾ cup mixed vegetables (white mushrooms, green onions, red pepper)

- ¼ cup mixed cheddar and mozzarella cheese

- 1 tsp. freshly chopped mixed herbs (cilantro and chives)

- Salt and freshly ground pepper to taste

Directions:

1. Combine the eggs and milk in a medium bowl, then add in the remaining ingredients apart from the cheese and mixed herbs, and beat well using a fork.

2. Pour the egg mixture into an evenly greased pan, then place it in the basket of your air fryer toast oven.

3. Cook for roughly 10 minutes at 350°F or until done to desire.

4. Sprinkle the cheese and mixed herbs on the omelet halfway through cook time.

5. Gently loosen the omelet from the sides of the pan using a spatula.

6. Serve hot!

Nutrition:

- Calories: 411

- Carbs: 14 g

- Fat: 33 g

- Protein: 28 g

9. Crunchy Zucchini Hash Browns

Preparation Time: 30 minutes

Cooking time: 15 minutes

Servings: 3

Ingredients:

- 4 medium zucchinis, peeled and grated

- 1 tsp. onion powder

- 1 tsp. garlic powder

- 2 tbsp. almond flour

- 1 ½ tsp. chili flakes

- Salt and freshly ground pepper to taste

- 2 tsp. olive oil

Directions:

1. Put the grated zucchini in between layers of kitchen towel and squeeze to drain excess water. Pour 1 teaspoon of oil in a pan, preferably non-stick, over medium heat and sauté the potatoes for about 3 minutes.

2. Transfer the zucchini to a shallow bowl and let cool. Sprinkle it with the remaining ingredients and mix it until it forms a proper mixture.

3. Transfer the zucchini mixture to a flat plate and pat it down to make 1 compact layer. Put it in the fridge and let it sit for 20 minutes.

4. Set your air fryer toast oven to 360°F.

5. Meanwhile, take out the flattened zucchini and divide into equal portions using a knife or cookie cutter.

6. Lightly brush your air fryer toast oven's basket with the remaining teaspoon of olive oil.

7. Gently place the zucchini pieces into the greased basket and fry for 12-15 minutes, flipping the hash browns halfway through.

8. Enjoy hot!

Nutrition:

- Calories: 195 Carbs: 14 g

- Fat: 11 g

- Protein: 6 g

10.   Crunchy Hash Browns

Preparation Time: 30 minutes

Cooking time: 15 minutes

Servings: 3

Ingredients:

- 5 medium potatoes, peeled and grated

- 1 tsp. onion powder 1 tsp. garlic powder

- 2 tbsp. corn flour

- 1 ½ tsp. chili flakes

- Salt and freshly ground pepper to taste

- 2 tsp. olive oil

Directions:

1. Put the grated potatoes in a large bowl and cover with ice-cold water and let it sit for a minute. Drain the water and repeat this step two times. (This removes the excess starch)

2. Pour 1 teaspoon of oil in a pan, preferably non-stick, over medium heat and sauté the potatoes for about 3 minutes.

3. Transfer the potatoes to a shallow bowl and let cool. Sprinkle the potatoes with the remaining ingredients and mix until it combines well.

4. Transfer the potato mix to a flat plate and pat it down to make 1 compact layer. Put it in the fridge and let it sit for 20 minutes.

5. Set your air fryer toast oven to 360°F.

6. Meanwhile, take out the flattened potato and divide it into equal portions using a knife or cookie cutter.

7. Lightly brush your air fryer toast oven's basket with the remaining teaspoon of olive oil.

8. Gently place the potato pieces into the greased basket and fry for 12-15 minutes, flipping the hash browns halfway through.

9. Enjoy hot!

Nutrition:

- Calories: 295 Carbs: 69 g

- Fat: 7 g Protein: 6 g

11.　Meaty Breakfast Omelet

Preparation Time: 10 minutes

Cooking time: 10 minutes

Servings: 2

Ingredients:

- 3 large eggs

- 100g ham, cut into small pieces

- ¼ cup milk

- ¾ cup mixed vegetables (mushrooms, scallions, bell pepper)

- ¼ cup mixed cheddar and mozzarella cheese

- 1 tsp. mixed herbs

- Salt and freshly ground pepper to taste

Directions:

1. Combine the eggs and milk in a medium bowl, then add in the remaining ingredients apart from the cheese and mixed herbs, and beat well using a fork.

2. Pour the egg mixture into an evenly greased pan, then place it in the basket of your air fryer toast oven.

3. Cook for roughly 10 minutes at 350°F or until done to desire.

4. Sprinkle the cheese and mixed herbs on the omelet halfway through cook time.

5. Gently loosen the omelet from the sides of the pan using a spatula.

6. Serve hot!

Nutrition:

- Calories: 278

- Carbs: 3 g Fat: 6 g

- Protein: 21 g

12.   Citrus Blueberry Muffins

Preparation Time: 15 minutes

Cooking time: 15 minutes

Servings: 3-4

Ingredients:

- 2 ½ cups cake flour

- ½ cup sugar

- ¼ cup light cooking oil such as avocado oil

- ½ cup heavy cream

- 1 cup fresh blueberries

- 2 eggs

- Zest and juice from 1 orange

- 1 tsp. pure vanilla extract

- 1 tsp. brown sugar for topping

Directions:

1. Start by combining the oil, heavy cream, eggs, orange juice, and

   vanilla extract in a large bowl, then set aside.

2. Separately combine the flour and sugar until evenly mixed, then pour little by little into the wet ingredients.

3. Combine until well blended but be careful not to over-mix.

4. Preheat your air fryer toast oven at 320°F

5. Gently fold the blueberries into the batter and divide them into cupcake holders, preferably, silicone cupcake holders, as you won't have to grease them. Alternatively, you can use cupcake paper liners on any cupcake holder/tray you could be having.

6. Sprinkle the tops with brown sugar and pop the muffins in the fryer.

7. Bake for about 12 minutes. Use a toothpick to check for readiness. When the muffins have evenly browned and an inserted toothpick comes out clean, they are ready.

8. Take out the muffins and let them cool.

9. Enjoy!

Nutrition:

- Calories: 289 Carbs: 18 g Fat: 32 g

- Protein: 21 g

CHAPTER 3:

Rice and Grains Recipes

13.   Garlic Black Beans and Potatoes

Preparation time: 10 minutes

Cooking time: 30 minutes

Servings: 4

Ingredients:

- 2 cups canned black beans, drained and rinsed

- 1-pound sweet potatoes, peeled and cubed

- 1 teaspoon chili powder

- ¼ cup veggie stock

- 1 teaspoon curry powder

- 1 tablespoon olive oil

- 4 garlic cloves, minced

- Salt and white pepper to the taste

Directions:

1. In the air fryer pan, mix the beans with the sweet potatoes and the other ingredients, toss, put the pan in the machine and cook at 370 degrees F for 30 minutes.

2. Divide between plates and serve.

Nutrition:

- Calories: 182

- Fat: 3 g

- Fiber: 6 g

- Carbs: 8 g

- Protein: 3 g

14. Beans and Corn

Preparation time: 10 minutes

Cooking time: 30 minutes

Servings: 4

Ingredients:

- 1 cup canned black beans, drained and rinsed

- 1 cup canned red kidney beans, drained and rinsed

- 1 cup corn

- 1 cup tomato sauce

- ½ cup cilantro, chopped

- 2 teaspoons chili powder

- 1 teaspoon garlic powder

- A pinch of salt and black pepper

Directions:

1. In the air fryer pan, mix the beans with the corn and the other ingredients, toss, introduce in your fryer and cook at 350 degrees F for 30 minutes.

2. Divide between plates and serve.

Nutrition:

- Calories: 365

- Fat: 12 g

- Fiber: 6 g

- Carbs: 22 g

- Protein: 26 g

15.　Corn and Pine Nuts Mix

Preparation time: 10 minutes

Cooking time: 20 minutes

Servings: 4

Ingredients:

- 2 cups corn ¼ cup pine nuts, toasted

- Juice of 1 lime Salt and black pepper to the taste

- 1 cup heavy cream 2 teaspoons olive oil

Directions:

1. In your air fryer pan, mix the corn with the pine nuts and the other ingredients, toss, put the pan in the machine and cook at 380 degrees F for 25 minutes.

2. Divide among plates and serve as a side dish.

Nutrition:

- Calories: 152 Fat: 3 g Fiber: 6 g

- Carbs: 7 g

- Protein: 4 g

CHAPTER 4:

Snacks and Appetizer

16.   Spicy Chickpeas

Preparation time: 5 minutes

Cooking time: 10 minutes

Servings: 4

Ingredients:

- 1 (15-ounce) can chickpeas, rinsed and drained

- 1 tablespoon olive oil

- ½ teaspoon ground cumin

- ½ teaspoon cayenne pepper

- ½ teaspoon smoked paprika

- Salt, as required

Directions:

1. In a bowl, add all the ingredients and toss to coat well.

2. Arrange the chickpeas in a basket.

3. Select "Air Fry" of Iconites Air Fryer Toaster Oven and then adjust the temperature to 390 degrees F.

4. Set the timer for 10 minutes and press "Start" to preheat.

5. After preheating, insert the basket in the oven.

6. When cooking time is complete, remove the basket from the oven and set it aside to cool slightly.

7. Serve warm.

Nutrition:

- Calories: 146 Total Fat: 5 g Saturated Fat: 5 g

- Cholesterol: 0 mg Sodium 66 mg Total Carbs: 18 g

- Fiber: 6 g Sugar 1 g Protein: 3 g

17.   Tortilla Chips

Preparation time: 10 minutes

Cooking time: 3 minutes

Servings: 3

Ingredients:

- 4 corn tortillas, cut into triangles

- 1 tablespoon olive oil

- Salt, to taste

Directions:

1. Coat the tortilla chips with oil and then sprinkle each side of the tortillas with salt.

2. Arrange the tortilla chips in the basket.

3. Select "Air Fry" of Iconites Air Fryer Toaster Oven and then adjust the temperature to 390 degrees F.

4. Set the timer for 3 minutes and press "Start" to preheat.

5. After preheating, insert the basket in the oven.

6. When cooking time is complete, remove the basket from the oven

   and serve warm.

Nutrition:

- Calories: 110

- Total Fat: 6 g

- Saturated Fat: 8 g

- Cholesterol: 0 mg

- Sodium: 65 mg

- Total Carbs: 13 g

- Fiber: 2 g

- Sugar: 3 g

- Protein: 8 g

18.   Feta Tater Tots

Preparation time: 15 minutes

Cooking time: 25 minutes

Servings: 6

Ingredients:

- 2 pounds frozen tater tots

- ½ cup feta cheese, crumbled

- ½ cup tomato, chopped

- ¼ cup black olives, pitted and sliced

- ¼ cup red onion, chopped

Directions:

1. Arrange the tater tots in the basket.

2. Select "Air Fry" of Iconites Air Fryer Toaster Oven and then adjust

   the temperature to 450 degrees F.

3. Set the timer for 15 minutes and press "Start" to preheat.

4. After preheating, insert the basket in the oven.

5. When cooking time is complete, remove the basket from the oven and transfer tots into a large bowl.

6. Add the feta cheese, tomatoes, olives, and onion and toss to coat well.

7. Now, place the mixture into a baking pan.

8. Select "Air Fry" of Iconites Air Fryer Toaster Oven and then adjust the temperature to 450 degrees F.

9. Set the timer for 10 minutes and press "Start" to preheat.

10. After preheating, insert the baking pan in the oven.

11. When cooking time is complete, remove the baking pan from the oven and serve warm.

Nutrition: Calories: 322 Total Fat: 17 g

- Saturated Fat: 6 g Cholesterol: 11 mg

- Sodium: 784 mg Total Carbs: 39 g

- Fiber: 1 g Sugar: 2 g

- Protein: 5 g

19. Cauliflower Poppers

Preparation time: 10 minutes

Cooking time: 20 minutes

Servings: 6

Ingredients:

- 3 tablespoons olive oil

- 1 teaspoon paprika

- ½ teaspoon ground cumin

- ¼ teaspoon ground turmeric

- Salt and ground black pepper, as required

- 1 medium head cauliflower, cut into florets

Directions:

1. In a bowl, place all ingredients and toss to coat well.

2. Place the cauliflower mixture in the greased baking pan.

3. Select "Bake" of Iconites Air Fryer Toaster Oven and then adjust the temperature to 450 degrees F.

4. Set the timer for 20 minutes and press "Start" to preheat.

5. After preheating, insert the baking pan in the oven.

6. Flip the cauliflower mixture once halfway through.

7. When cooking time is complete, remove the pan from the oven and serve warm.

Nutrition:

- Calories: 73

- Total Fat: 1 g

- Saturated Fat: 1 g

- Cholesterol: 0 mg

- Sodium: 41 mg

- Total Carbs: 7 g

- Fiber: 3 g

- Sugar: 1 g

- Protein: 1 g

20.   Fish Nuggets

Preparation time: 15 minutes

Cooking time: 8 minutes

Servings: 5

Ingredients:

- 1 cup all-purpose flour

- 2 eggs

- ¾ cup seasoned breadcrumbs

- 2 tablespoons vegetable oil

- 1-pound boneless haddock fillet, cut into strips

Directions:

1. In a shallow dish, place the flour.

2. In a second dish, crack the eggs and beat well.

3. In a third dish, mix the breadcrumbs and oil.

4. Coat the nuggets with flour, then dip into beaten eggs, and finally, coat with the breadcrumbs.

5. Place the nuggets into the greased basket in a single layer.

6. Select "Air Fry" of Iconites Air Fryer Toaster Oven and then adjust the temperature to 390 degrees F.

7. Set the timer for 8 minutes and press "Start" to preheat.

8. After preheating, insert the basket in the center position of the oven.

9. Flip the nuggets once halfway through.

10. When cooking time is complete, remove the basket from the oven.

11. Serve warm.

Nutrition:

- Calories: 311 Total Fat: 14 g

- Saturated Fat: 7 g

- Cholesterol: 110 mg

- Sodium: 312 mg

- Total Carbs: 24 g

- Fiber: 3 g

- Sugar 2 g

- Protein: 26 g

21.   Buffalo Chicken Wings

Preparation time: 15 minutes

Cooking time: 19 minutes

Servings: 4

Ingredients:

- 1½ pounds chicken wings

- 1 teaspoon olive oil

- Salt and ground black pepper, as required

- ¼ cup buffalo sauce

Directions:

1. In a large bowl, mix the chicken wings, oil, salt, and black pepper.

2. Arrange the wings into a greased baking pan.

3. Select "Air Fry" of Iconites Air Fryer Toaster Oven and then adjust the temperature to 360 degrees F.

4. Set the timer for 19 minutes and press "Start" to preheat.

5. After preheating, insert the baking pan in the oven.

6. Flip the chicken wings once halfway through and coat with buffalo sauce.

7. When cooking time is complete, remove the pan from the oven and serve immediately.

Nutrition:

- Calories: 334

- Total Fat: 18 g

- Saturated Fat: 6 g

- Cholesterol: 151 mg

- Sodium: 209 mg

- Total Carbs: 1 g

- Fiber: 0 g

- Sugar: 0 g

- Protein: 42 g

CHAPTER 5:

Vegan Recipes

22.   Spicy Asian Brussels Sprouts

Preparation Time: 10 minutes

Cooking Time: 15 minutes

Servings: 4

Ingredients:

- 1 lb. Brussels sprouts, cut in half (1 green)

- 1 tbsp gochujang (1/2 condiment)

- 1 1/2 tbsp olive oil (1/4 condiment)

- 1/2 tsp salt (1/4 condiment)

Directions:

1.   In a bowl, mix olive oil, gochujang, and salt.

2.   Add Brussels sprouts into the bowl and toss until well coated.

3. Add Brussels sprouts into the air fryer basket and cook at 360 F for

   15 minutes.

4. Serve and enjoy.

Nutrition

- Calories: 94 Fat: 5 g Protein: 4 g

23. Healthy Mushrooms

Preparation Time: 10 minutes

Cooking Time: 12 minutes

Servings: 2

Ingredients:

- 8 oz mushrooms, clean and cut into quarters (2 healthy Fats)

- 1 tbsp fresh parsley, chopped (1/2 green)

- 1 tsp soy sauce (1/4 condiment)

- 1/2 tsp garlic powder (1/4 condiment)

- 1 tbsp olive oil (1/4 condiment)

- Pepper (1/8 condiment)

- Salt (1/8 condiment)

Directions:

1. Add mushrooms and remaining ingredients into the bowl and toss well.

2. Add mushrooms into the air fryer basket and cook at 380 F for 12 minutes. Stir halfway through.

3. Serve and enjoy.

Nutrition

- Calories: 90 Fat: 7g

- Protein: 4g

CHAPTER 6:

Quick and Easy Recipes

24.   Tuna Patties

Preparation Time: 10 minutes

Cooking Time: 10 minutes

Servings: 2

Ingredients:

- 2 cans tuna

- 1/2 lemon juice

- 1/2 tsp onion powder

- 1 tsp garlic powder

- 1/2 tsp dried dill

- 1 1/2 tbsp. mayonnaise

- 1 1/2 tbsp. almond flour

- 1/4 tsp pepper

- 1/4 tsp salt

Directions:

1. Preheat the air fryer to 400 F.

2. Add all ingredients to a mixing bowl and mix until well combined.

3. Spray air fryer basket with cooking spray.

4. Make four patties from the mixture and place them in the air fryer basket.

5. Cook patties for 10 minutes at 400 F, if you want crispier patties, then cook for 3 minutes more.

6. Serve and enjoy.

Nutrition:

- Calories: 414

- Fat: 20.6 g Carbohydrates: 5.6 g Sugar: 1.3 g

- Protein: 48.8 g

- Cholesterol: 58 mg

25.   Crispy Fish Sticks

Preparation Time: 10 minutes

Cooking Time: 10 minutes

Servings: 4

Ingredients:

- 1 lb. white fish, cut into pieces

- 3/4 tsp Cajun seasoning

- 1 1/2 cups pork rind, crushed

- 2 tbsp. water

- 2 tbsp. Dijon mustard

- 1/4 cup mayonnaise

- Pepper

- Salt

Directions:

1. Spray air fryer basket with cooking spray.

2. In a small bowl, whisk together mayonnaise, water, and mustard.

3. In a shallow bowl, mix pork rind, pepper, Cajun seasoning, and salt.

4. Dip fish pieces in mayo mixture and coat with pork rind mixture and place in the air fryer basket.

5. Cook at 400 F for 5 minutes. Turn fish sticks to another side and cook for 5 minutes more.

6. Serve and enjoy.

Nutrition:

- Calories: 397

- Fat: 36.4 g

- Carbohydrates: 4 g

- Sugar: 1 g

- Protein: 14.7 g

- Cholesterol: 4 mg

26. Delicious White Fish

Preparation Time: 10 minutes

Cooking Time: 10 minutes

Servings: 2

Ingredients:

- 12 oz. white fish fillets

- 1/2 tsp onion powder

- 1/2 tsp lemon pepper seasoning

- 1/2 tsp garlic powder

- 1 tbsp. olive oil

- Pepper

- Salt

Directions:

1. Spray air fryer basket with cooking spray.

2. Preheat the air fryer to 360 F.

3. Coat fish fillets with olive oil and season with onion powder, lemon pepper seasoning, garlic powder, pepper, and salt.

4.   Place fish fillets in the air fryer basket and cook for 10-12 minutes.

5.   Serve and enjoy.

Nutrition:

- Calories: 358

- Fat: 19.8 g

- Carbohydrates: 1.3 g

- Sugar: 0.4 g

- Protein: 41.9 g

- Cholesterol: 131 mg

27. Salmon Patties

Preparation Time: 10 minutes

Cooking Time: 7 minutes

Servings: 2

Ingredients:

- 8 oz. salmon fillet, minced

- 1 lemon, sliced

- 1/2 tsp garlic powder

- 1 egg, lightly beaten

- 1/8 tsp salt

Directions:

1. Add all ingredients except lemon slices into the bowl and mix until well combined.

2. Spray air fryer basket with cooking spray.

3. Place lemon slice into the air fryer basket.

4. Make the equal shape of patties from salmon mixture and place on top of lemon slices into the air fryer basket.

5. Cook at 390 F for 7 minutes.

6. Serve and enjoy.

Nutrition:

- Calories: 184

- Fat: 9.2 g

- Carbohydrates: 1 g

- Sugar: 0.4 g

- Protein: 24.9 g

- Cholesterol: 132 mg

CHAPTER 7:

Beef, Pork, & Lamb Recipes

27.   Crisp Pork Chops

Preparation Time: 10 minutes

Cooking Time: 12 minutes

Servings: 6

Ingredients:

- 1 1/2 lbs. pork chops, boneless

- 1 tsp paprika

- 1 tsp creole seasoning

- 1 tsp garlic powder

- 1/4 cup parmesan cheese, grated

- 1/3 cup almond flour

Directions:

1.   Preheat the air fryer to 360 F.

2. Add all ingredients except pork chops in a zip-lock bag.

3. Add pork chops to the bag. Seal bag and shake well to coat pork chops.

4. Remove pork chops from zip-lock bag and place in the air fryer basket.

5. Cook pork chops for 10-12 minutes.

6. Serve and enjoy.

Nutrition:

- Calories: 230 Fat: 11 g Carbohydrates: 2 g

- Sugar: 0.2 g

- Protein: 27 g

- Cholesterol: 79 mg

28. Parmesan Pork Chops

Preparation Time: 10 minutes

Cooking Time: 15 minutes

Servings: 4

Ingredients:

- 4 pork chops, boneless

- 4 tbsp parmesan cheese, grated

- 1 cup pork rind

- 3 eggs, lightly beaten

- 1/2 tsp chili powder

- 1/2 tsp onion powder

- 1 tsp paprika

- 1/4 tsp pepper

- 1/2 tsp salt

Directions:

1. Preheat the air fryer to 400 F.

2. Season pork chops with pepper and salt.

3. Add pork rind in the food processor and process until crumbs form.

4. Mix pork rind crumbs and seasoning in a large bowl.

5. Place egg in a separate bowl.

6. Dip pork chops in egg mixture, then coat with pork crumb mixture and place in the air fryer basket.

7. Cook pork chops for 12-15 minutes.

8. Serve and enjoy.

Nutrition:

- Calories: 329

- Fat: 24 g

- Carbohydrates: 1 g

- Sugar: 0.4 g

- Protein: 23 g

- Cholesterol: 158 mg

29.   Meatloaf Sliders

Preparation Time: 10 minutes

Cooking Time: 10 minutes

Servings: 8

Ingredients:

- 1 lb. ground beef

- 1/2 tsp dried tarragon

- 1 tsp Italian seasoning

- 1 tbsp Worcestershire sauce

- 1/4 cup ketchup

- 1/4 cup coconut flour

- 1/2 cup almond flour

- 1 garlic clove, minced

- 1/4 cup onion, chopped

- 2 eggs, lightly beaten

- 1/4 tsp pepper

- 1/2 tsp sea salt

Directions:

1. Add all ingredients into the mixing bowl and mix until well combined.

2. Make the equal shape of patties from the mixture and place them on a plate. Place in refrigerator for 10 minutes.

3. Spray air fryer basket with cooking spray.

4. Preheat the air fryer to 360° F.

5. Place prepared patties in air fryer basket and cook for 10 minutes.

6. Serve and enjoy.

Nutrition:

- Calories: 228 Fat: 16 g

- Carbohydrates: 6 g

- Sugar: 2 g

- Protein: 13 g

- Cholesterol: 80 mg

30. Quick & Easy Steak

Preparation Time: 10 minutes

Cooking Time: 7 minutes

Servings: 2

Ingredients:

- 12 oz steaks

- 1/2 tbsp unsweetened cocoa powder

- 1 tbsp Montreal steak seasoning

- 1 tsp liquid smoke

- 1 tbsp soy sauce

- Pepper

- Salt

Directions:

1. Add steak, liquid smoke, and soy sauce in a zip-lock bag and shake well.

2. Season steak with seasonings and place in the refrigerator overnight.

3. Place marinated steak in air fryer basket and cook at 375 F for 5 minutes.

4. Turn steak to another side and cook for 2 minutes more.

5. Serve and enjoy.

Nutrition:

- Calories: 356

- Fat: 8.7 g

- Carbohydrates: 1.4 g

- Sugar: 0.2 g

- Protein: 62.2 g

- Cholesterol: 153 mg

31.   Perfect Cheeseburger

Preparation Time: 5 minutes

Cooking Time: 12 minutes

Servings: 2

Ingredients:

- 1/2 lb. ground beef

- 1/4 tsp onion powder

- 2 cheese slices

- 1/4 tsp pepper

- 1/8 tsp salt

Directions:

1. In a bowl, mix ground beef, onion powder, pepper, and salt.

2. Make two equal shapes of patties from the meat mixture and place them in the air fryer basket.

3. Cook patties at 370° F for 12 minutes. Turn patties halfway through.

4. Once the air fryer timer goes off, place cheese slices on top of each patty and close the air fryer basket for 1 minute.

5. Serve and enjoy.

Nutrition:

- Calories: 325

- Fat: 16.4 g

- Carbohydrates: 0.8 g

- Sugar: 0.3 g

- Protein: 41.4 g

- Cholesterol: 131 mg

32.   Steak Bites with Mushrooms

Preparation Time: 10 minutes

Cooking Time: 18 minutes

Servings: 3

Ingredients:

- 1 lb. steaks, cut into 1/2-inch cubes

- 1/2 tsp garlic powder

- 1 tsp Worcestershire sauce

- tbsp butter, melted

- 8 oz mushrooms, sliced

- Pepper

- Salt

Directions:

1. Add all ingredients into the large mixing bowl and toss well.

2. Spray air fryer basket with cooking spray.

3. Preheat the air fryer to 400 F.

4.   Add steak mushroom mixture into the air fryer basket and cook at

400 F for 15-18 minutes. Shake basket twice.

5.   Serve and enjoy.

Nutrition:

- Calories: 388

- Fat: 15.5 g

- Carbohydrates: 3.2 g

- Sugar: 1.8 g

- Protein: 57.1 g

- Cholesterol: 156 mg

CHAPTER 8:

Poultry Recipes

33.   Chicken Popcorn

Preparation Time: 10 minutes

Cooking time: 10 minutes

Servings: 6

Ingredients:

- 4 eggs

- 11/2 lbs. chicken breasts, cut into small chunks

- 1 tsp paprika

- 1/2 tsp garlic powder

- 1 tsp onion powder

- 11/2 cups pork rind, crushed

- 1/4 cup coconut flour

- Pepper

- Salt

Directions:

1. In a small bowl, mix coconut flour, pepper, and salt.

2. In another bowl, whisk eggs until combined.

3. Take one more bowl and mix pork panko, paprika, garlic powder, and onion powder.

4. Add chicken pieces to a large mixing bowl. Sprinkle coconut flour mixture over chicken and toss well.

5. Dip chicken pieces in the egg mixture and coat with pork panko mixture and place on a plate.

6. Spray air fryer basket with cooking spray.

7. Preheat the air fryer to 400 F.

8. Add half prepared chicken to the air fryer basket and cook for 10-12 minutes. Shake basket halfway through.

9. Cook the remaining half using the same method.

10. Serve and enjoy.

Nutrition:

- Calories: 265

- Fat: 11 g

- Carbohydrates: 3 g

- Sugar: 5 g

- Protein: 35 g

- Cholesterol: 195 mg

34. Delicious Whole Chicken

Preparation Time: 10 minutes

Cooking time: 50 minutes

Servings: 4

Ingredients:

- 3 lbs. whole chicken, remove giblets, and pat dry chicken

- 1 tsp Italian seasoning

- 1/2 tsp garlic powder

- 1/2 tsp onion powder

- 1/4 tsp paprika

- 1/4 tsp pepper

- 11/2 tsp salt

Directions:

1. In a small bowl, mix Italian seasoning, garlic powder, onion powder, paprika, pepper, and salt.

2. Rub spice mixture from inside and outside of the chicken.

3. Place chicken breast side down in air fryer basket.

4. Roast chicken for 30 minutes at 360° F.

5. Turn chicken and roast for 20 minutes more or internal temperature

   of the chicken reaches 165° F.

6. Serve and enjoy.

Nutrition:

- Calories: 356

- Fat: 25 g

- Carbohydrates: 1 g

- Sugar: 1 g

- Protein: 30 g

- Cholesterol: 120 mg

35.   Lemon Pepper Chicken Wings

Preparation Time: 10 minutes

Cooking time: 16 minutes

Servings: 4

Ingredients:

- 1 lb. chicken wings 1 tsp lemon pepper 1 tbsp olive oil

- 1 tsp salt

Directions:

1. Add chicken wings into the large mixing bowl.

2. Add remaining ingredients over chicken and toss well to coat.

3. Place chicken wings in the air fryer basket.

4. Cook chicken wings for 8 minutes at 400 F.

5. Turn chicken wings to another side and cook for 8 minutes more.

6. Serve and enjoy.

Nutrition:

- Calories: 247 Fat: 11 g Carbohydrates: 3 g Sugar: 0 g

- Protein: 32 g Cholesterol: 101 mg

36. BBQ Chicken Wings

Preparation Time: 10 minutes

Cooking time: 20 minutes

Servings: 4

Ingredients:

- 11/2 lbs. chicken wings

- 1 tbsp unsweetened BBQ sauce

- 1 tsp paprika

- 1 tbsp olive oil

- 1 tsp garlic powder

- Pepper

- Salt

Directions:

1. In a large bowl, toss chicken wings with garlic powder, oil, paprika, pepper, and salt.

2. Preheat the air fryer to 360° F.

3. Add chicken wings to the air fryer basket and cook for 12 minutes.

4. Turn chicken wings to another side and cook for 5 minutes more.

5. Remove chicken wings from air fryer and toss with BBQ sauce.

6. Return chicken wings to the air fryer basket and cook for 2 minutes more.

7. Serve and enjoy.

Nutrition:

- Calories: 372

- Fat: 12 g

- Carbohydrates: 3 g

- Sugar: 7 g

- Protein: 44 g

- Cholesterol: 151 mg

37. Flavorful Fried Chicken

Preparation Time: 10 minutes

Cooking time: 40 minutes

Servings: 10

Ingredients:

- 5 lbs. chicken, about 10 pieces

- 1 tbsp coconut oil

- 11/2 tsp white pepper

- 1 tsp ground ginger

- 1 1/2 tsp garlic salt

- 1 tbsp paprika

- 1 tsp dried mustard

- 1 tsp pepper

- 1 tsp celery salt

- 1/3 tsp oregano

- 1/2 tsp basil

- 1/2 tsp thyme

- 1 cups pork rind, crushed

- 1 tbsp vinegar

- 1 cup unsweetened almond milk

- 1/2 tsp salt

Directions:

1. Add chicken to a large mixing bowl.

2. Add milk and vinegar over chicken and place in the refrigerator for 2 hours.

3. In a shallow dish, mix pork rinds, white pepper, ginger, garlic, paprika, mustard, pepper, celery salt, oregano, basil, thyme, and salt.

4. Coat air fryer basket with coconut oil.

5. Coat each chicken piece with pork rind mixture and place on a plate.

6. Place half coated chicken in the air fryer basket.

7. Cook chicken at 360° F for 10 minutes, then turn chicken to another side and cook for 10 minutes more or until internal temperature reaches 165 F.

8. Cook remaining chicken using the same method.

9. Serve and enjoy.

Nutrition:

- Calories: 539

- Fat: 37 g

- Carbohydrates: 1 g

- Sugar: 0 g

- Protein: 45 g

- Cholesterol: 175 mg

CHAPTER 9:

Fish and Seafood Recipes

38.   Grilled Salmon

Preparation Time: 5 minutes

Cooking time: 10 minutes

Servings: 3

Ingredients

- 2 Salmon Fillets

- 1/2 Tsp Lemon Pepper

- 1/2 Tsp Garlic Powder

- Salt and Pepper

- 1/3 Cup Soy Sauce

- 1/3 Cup Sugar

- 2 Tbsp Olive Oil

Directions:

1. Season salmon fillets with lemon pepper, garlic powder, and salt. In a shallow bowl, add a third cup of water and combine the olive oil, soy sauce, and sugar. Place salmon in the bowl and immerse in the sauce. Cover with cling film and allow to marinate in the refrigerator for at least an hour.

2. Preheat the Chefman Air Fryer Oven at 350 degrees F.

3. Place salmon into the air fryer and cook for 10 minutes or more until the fish is tender.

4. Serve with lemon wedges

Nutrition:

- Calories: 213 Fat: 8g

- Protein: 15g Sugar: 3g

39.　Sweet and Savory Breaded Shrimp

Preparation Time: 5 minutes

Cooking time: 20 minutes

Servings: 2

Ingredients

- ½ pound of fresh shrimp, peeled from their shells and rinsed

- 2 raw eggs

- ½ cup of breadcrumbs (we like Panko, but any brand or home recipe will do)

- ½ white onion, peeled and rinsed and finely chopped

- 1 teaspoon of ginger-garlic paste

- ½ teaspoon of turmeric powder

- ½ teaspoon of red chili powder

- ½ teaspoon of cumin powder

- ½ teaspoon of black pepper powder

- ½ teaspoon of dry mango powder

- Pinch of salt

Directions:

1. Cover the basket of the air fryer with a lining of tin foil, leaving the edges uncovered to allow air to circulate through the basket.

2. Preheat the Chefman Air Fryer Oven to 350 degrees F.

3. In a large mixing bowl, beat the eggs until fluffy and until the yolks and whites are fully combined.

4. Dunk all the shrimp in the egg mixture, fully submerging.

5. In a separate mixing bowl, combine the bread crumbs with all the dry ingredients until evenly blended.

6. One by one, coat the egg-covered shrimp in the mixed dry ingredients so that is fully covered, and place on the foil-lined air-fryer basket.

7. Set the Chefman Air Fryer Oven timer to 20 minutes.

8. Halfway through the cooking time, shake the handle of the air-fryer so that the breaded shrimp jostles inside and fry-coverage is even.

9. After 20 minutes, when the fryer shuts off, the shrimp will be perfectly cooked and their breaded crust golden-brown and

delicious! Using tongs, remove from the air fryer and set on a serving dish to cool.

Nutrition:

- Calories: 213 Fat: 8g

- Protein: 15g Sugar: 3g

CHAPTER 10:

Sweet and Dessert Recipes

40.   Lemon Sole and Swiss chard

Preparation time: 10 minutes

Cooking time: 14 minutes

Servings: 4

Ingredients:

- 1 teaspoon lemon zest, grated

- 4 white bread slices, quartered

- ¼ cup walnuts, chopped

- ¼ cup parmesan, grated

- 4 tablespoons olive oil

- 4 sole fillets, boneless

- Salt and black pepper to the taste

- 4 tablespoons butter

- ¼ cup lemon juice

- 1 tablespoons caper

- 1 garlic clove, minced

- 2 bunches Swiss chard, chopped

Directions:

1. In your food processor, mix bread with walnuts, cheese, and lemon zest and pulse well.

2. Add half of the olive oil, pulse well again and leave aside for now.

3. Heat a pan with the butter over medium heat, add lemon juice, salt, pepper, and capers, stir well, add fish and toss it.

4. Transfer fish to your preheated air fryer basket, top with bread mix you've made at the beginning, and cook at 350 degrees F for 14 minutes.

5. Meanwhile, heat another pan with the rest of the oil, add garlic, Swiss chard, salt, and pepper, stir gently, cook for 2 minutes and take off the heat.

6. Divide fish among plates and serve with sautéed chard on the side.

7. Enjoy!

Nutrition:

- Calories: 321

- Fat: 7 g

- Fiber: 18 g

- Carbs: 27 g

- Protein: 12 g

Conclusion

The recipes and suggestions given are intended to help you make informed decisions about your health. Maintaining a healthy diet means making the right choices for you. What works for some may not work for you and that's ok. It has taken us a long time to get to where we are, and with that in mind, we may not be the best teachers or the best at presenting information on how to make decisions for yourself. Our goal is simply to help you be healthier and, above all, happy! In short, this cookbook is designed so that you have no excuse not to eat better. All the recipes are easy and inexpensive to make. I hope you have enjoyed reading this book as much as I have enjoyed writing it.

This cookbook contains not only recipes, but also information about air fryers and how to use them properly. We recommend referencing the included cookbook guide before each recipe to ensure that you're following the instructions correctly. As you've seen from these recipes, there is no shortage of ingredients that can be air fried. Everything from chicken to steak and from shrimp to garlic bread can be cooked in an air fryer, making this appliance a staple in any kitchen.

If you're looking to buy an air fryer but are feeling intimidated by all the different brands, you can check out our air fryer evaluations to find out which models are best for your needs. We've tested and studied numerous models on the market, so we know what's good and what's not so well. There are many reasons to own an air fryer, but there are some things you should know before buying yours. These tips will help you in deciding which type of air fryer is right for you. Air Fryers come in a few different types, including convection and traditional models, so be sure to learn about your specific model before making the purchase.

There are many reasons to own an air fryer, but there are some things you should know before buying yours. I hope this cookbook has been helpful to you. I've tried to cover a variety of dishes with recipes that are easy to make and don't require a lot of fuss. The recipes in this book will help you learn how to use an air fryer so that you can indulge in delicious, healthy, homemade fries, wings, pizza crusts, or any other treats from the comfort of your own home without all the chemicals and oil.

CPSIA information can be obtained
at www.ICGtesting.com
Printed in the USA
BVHW041747220621
610214BV00012B/2442